Light and Color

by Vickey Herold

Table of Contents

Introduction

Light is **energy** from the sun. Light does many things. Color comes from light. Light is important for many reasons.

▲ Light is energy from the sun.

energy

lasers

particles

reflection

mirror

refraction

ultraviolet light

visible light

waves

white light

x-rays

See the Glossary
on page 30.

3

What Is Light?

Light is **particles** of energy. The particles are very tiny pieces of light.

Try This

1. Turn on a lamp.

2. Hold your hand close to the bulb.

3. Is your hand getting warm? The heat is energy from the light.

▲ Light is tiny particles of energy.

Particles flow from light. Particles flow from the sun.

▲ Particles of light flow from the sun.

Particles flow from a light bulb.

▲ Particles of light flow from a bulb.

Did You Know?

People studied light long ago. Sir Isaac Newton discovered particles of light. The year was 1687.

▲ Sir Isaac Newton

5

Particles travel in **waves**. The waves move like waves in water. The waves travel through space.

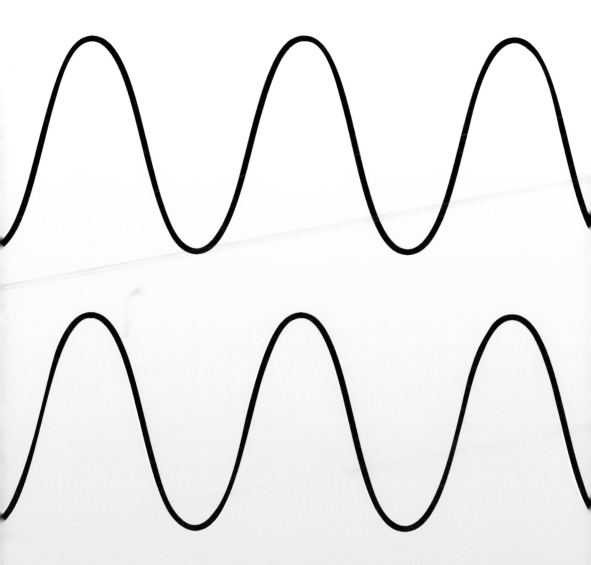

▲ **Light travels in waves.**

Light travels faster than all other things. Light travels about 186,000 miles (about 299,000 kilometers) per second. The sun is 93 million miles (150 million kilometers) from Earth. Sunlight reaches Earth in about eight minutes.

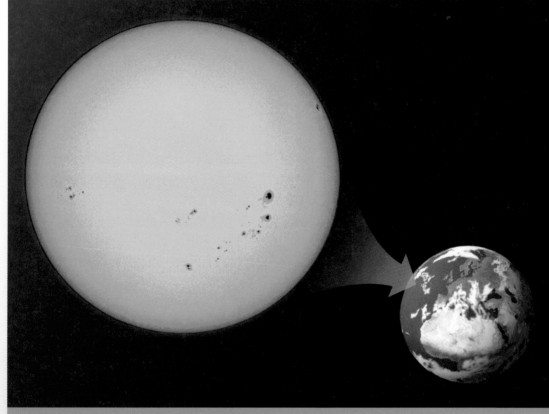

▲ **Light travels faster than other things.**

Solve This

Light travels 186,000 miles (about 299,000 kilometers) in one second. How far does light travel in half a second?

Answer: 93,000 miles (about 149,500 kilometers)

7

People do not see all waves of light. **X-rays** are waves of light. People do not see x-rays. Special film helps people see x-rays.

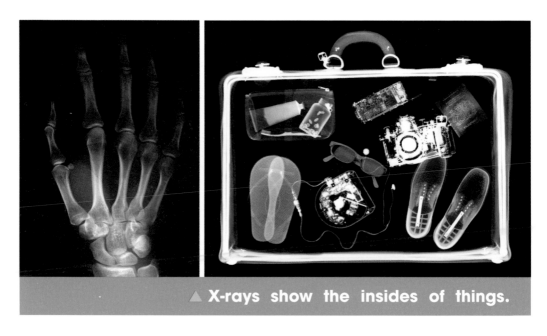

▲ X-rays show the insides of things.

People do not see **ultraviolet light**. Ultraviolet light causes sunburns.

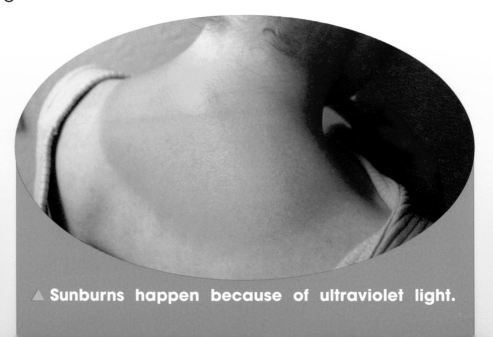

▲ Sunburns happen because of ultraviolet light.

Visible light is waves of light. People see visible light. Color comes from visible light.

light people can see

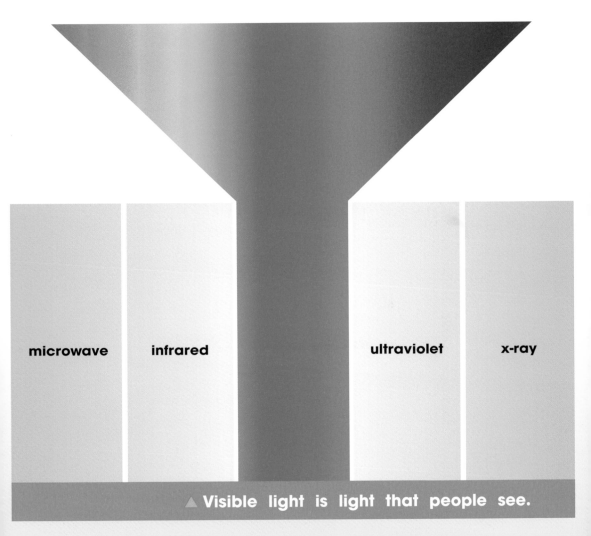

microwave   infrared   ultraviolet   x-ray

▲ Visible light is light that people see.

What Is Color?

Color is visible light from the sun. Visible waves of light make colors. Waves of light make different colors.

▲ Color is visible waves of light.

Waves of light are different lengths. Waves of different lengths make different colors. The color violet has the shortest wave. The color red has the longest wave.

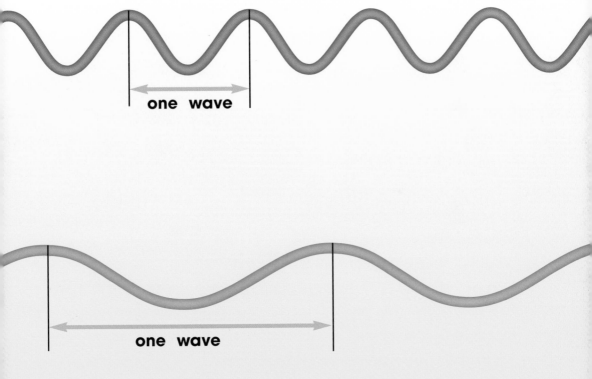

one wave

one wave

Light from the sun is **white light**. White light is all the colors mixed together. White light has waves of many different lengths. The waves split to make different colors.

▲ White light splits to make different colors.

White light splits into six main colors. All other colors come from six main colors. The colors are:

- **red**,
- **orange**,
- **yellow**,
- **green**,
- **blue**, and
- **violet**.

Reread

Reread pages 10–13. What do you know about color? What do you know about light and color?

▲ White light splits into six main colors.

Rainbows happen when white light passes through rain. Some drops of rain split white light. White light becomes waves of many lengths. Each length makes a different color. The different colors make a rainbow.

Did You Know?

Rainbows have all the colors of white light. The color red is usually on top. The color violet is usually on the bottom.

▲ White light makes a rainbow.

All rainbows have the same colors. People see rainbows. People often see rainbows after rain.

▲ **People see rainbows after rain.**

People often see rainbows in waterfalls.

▲ **Some rainbows are in waterfalls.**

What Does Light Do?

Light bounces. Light that bounces makes a **reflection**. Reflections happen when light bounces off things.

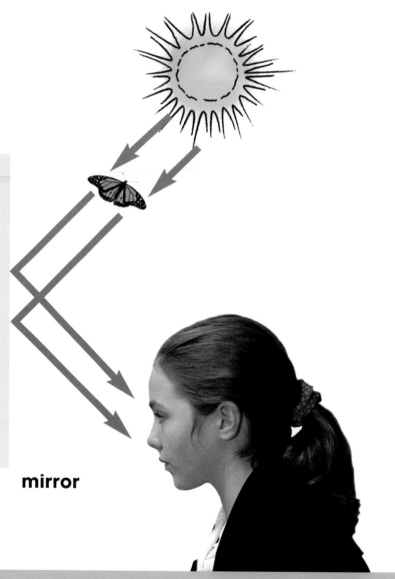

mirror

▲ A reflection is when light bounces off things.

You see yourself in a mirror because light bounces. Light bounces off your body. The light bounces to the mirror. Then you see a reflection in the mirror.

Light bends when it passes through things. **Refraction** happens when light bends. Light changes direction because of refraction.

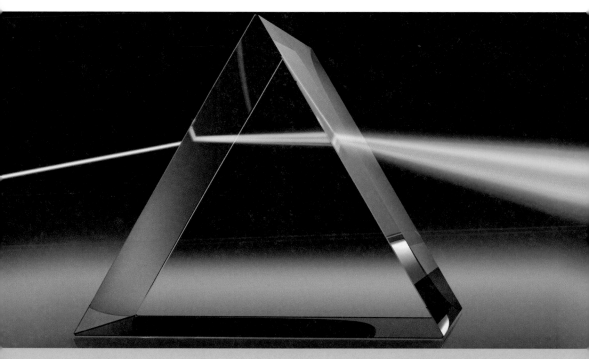

▲ **Light bends.**

Try This

See refraction!

1. Fill a glass half full with water.

2. Place a straw in the water.

3. Does the straw look broken?

Refraction causes white light to split. Colors happen when white light splits. Colors happen when light changes direction.

Reread

Reread pages 16–19. When do reflections happen? When does refraction happen?

▲ Refraction splits white light into different colors.

Light travels through some things. Light travels through glass. Light travels through windows.

▲ Light travels through things.

Light can not travel through some things. Some things block light. Things that block light have shadows. Buildings have shadows. People have shadows.

▲ **Buildings block light.**

It's a Fact

Shadows change when the sun moves. Shadows are short when the sun is high. Shadows are long when the sun is low.

▲ **People block light.**

Why Is Light Important?

People can not see without light. People can see because three things work together.

1 light

2 your eyes

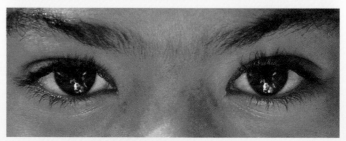

3 your brain

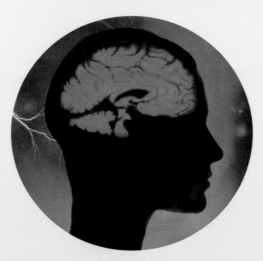

Light travels into your eyes. Your eyes turn the light into messages. The messages travel to your brain. Your brain turns the messages into pictures. Then you see.

▲ The light goes into your eyes.

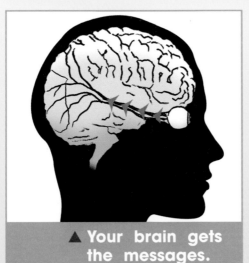

▲ Your brain gets the messages.

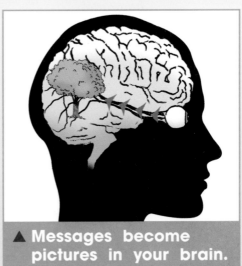

▲ Messages become pictures in your brain.

Light helps people in other ways, too. Plants need light to live. People need plants to live. People eat plants.

▲ **Plants need light.**

▲ **People eat plants.**

Plants help make the air people breathe.

▲ **Plants help people.**

Light is energy. Light makes heat. Light from the sun warms Earth.

▲ **Earth is warm because of the sun.**

It's a Fact

People make solar energy from the sun. People use solar energy to make machines move. Some cars use solar energy instead of gasoline.

25

People use light as a tool. **Lasers** are light. Lasers cut very hard things.

▲ **People use lasers to cut things.**

Did You Know?

Some lasers cut diamonds.
Some lasers cut steel.

Some lasers help doctors. Doctors use lasers to help people see better. Doctors use lasers to keep people safe.

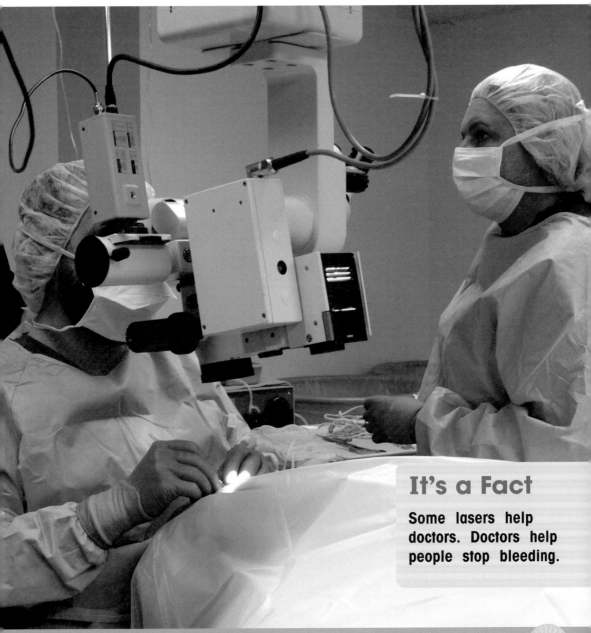

It's a Fact

Some lasers help doctors. Doctors help people stop bleeding.

▲ **Lasers can help doctors.**

Summary

Light is energy. Color comes from light. Light helps people in many ways. Light is important to people.

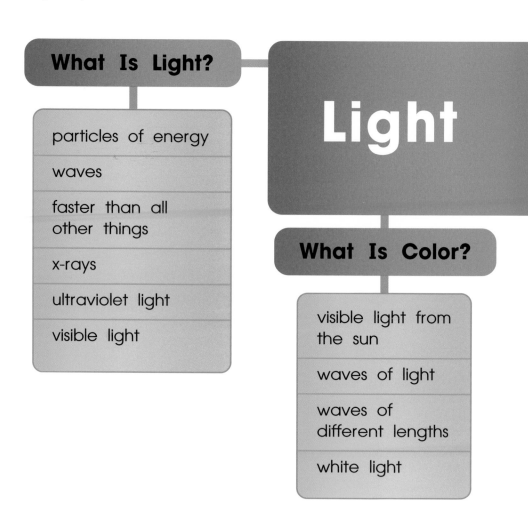

What Is Light?

- particles of energy
- waves
- faster than all other things
- x-rays
- ultraviolet light
- visible light

Light

What Is Color?

- visible light from the sun
- waves of light
- waves of different lengths
- white light

Why Is Light Important?

helps people see
helps plants
makes heat
for lasers

What Does Light Do?

bounces
bends
travels through some things
can not travel through some things

Think About It

1. What is light?
2. What is color?
3. Why is light important?

Glossary

energy power

*Light is **energy** from the sun.*

lasers tools that use light

Lasers cut very hard things.

particles very tiny pieces

*Light is **particles** of energy.*

mirror

reflection what happens when light bounces

*Light that bounces makes a **reflection**.*

refraction what happens when light bends

Refraction happens when light bends.

ultraviolet light a type of light that people do not see

*People do not see **ultraviolet light**.*

visible light light that people see

Visible light is waves of light.

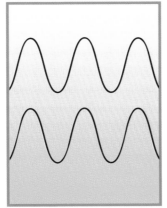

waves how light moves

*Particles travel in **waves**.*

white light visible light that splits into colors

*Light from the sun is **white light**.*

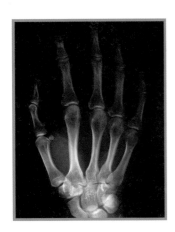

x-rays waves of light that people do not see

X-rays are waves of light.

Index